Right from the time of its foundation, nearly 1000 years ago, by monks who followed the Rule of St Benedict, this has been a special place of prayer and pilgrimage. We hope you too will be able to pray here.

In a way, the building says it all. The fortress-like architecture speaks of the strength of God, inviting our trust. The soft pink stone speaks of the loving tenderness of God for each and every one of us, inviting our response.

This is a living community of faith. It looks back with confidence to its continuity with the past, and it looks forward with hope to God's future. This is a living community, open to change, which exists to worship and serve the living God, and to serve the people of Chester and the city's many visitors.

We hope that our Cathedral will be a place where strangers are made welcome, seekers may find God, believers may grow in holiness, and Christians may engage with the issues of our times.

The Very Reverend Prof. Gordon McPhate
Dean of Chester

Welcome to Chester Cathedral

Contents

Right: A university graduation ceremony in the magnificent Nave of Chester Cathedral; daily worship takes place in the Cathedral, as well as many special services and events.

Cathedral Timeline

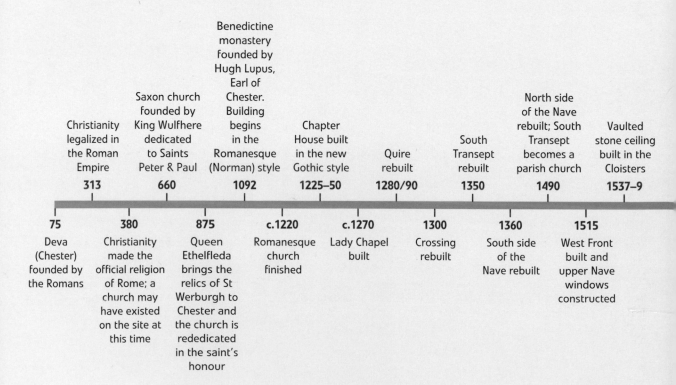

313	660	1092	1225–50	1280/90	1350	1490	1537–9
Christianity legalized in the Roman Empire	Saxon church founded by King Wulfhere dedicated to Saints Peter & Paul	Benedictine monastery founded by Hugh Lupus, Earl of Chester. Building begins in the Romanesque (Norman) style	Chapter House built in the new Gothic style	Quire rebuilt	South Transept rebuilt	North side of the Nave rebuilt; South Transept becomes a parish church	Vaulted stone ceiling built in the Cloisters

75	380	875	c.1220	c.1270	1300	1360	1515
Deva (Chester) founded by the Romans	Christianity made the official religion of Rome; a church may have existed on the site at this time	Queen Ethelfleda brings the relics of St Werburgh to Chester and the church is rededicated in the saint's honour	Romanesque church finished	Lady Chapel built	Crossing rebuilt	South side of the Nave rebuilt	West Front built and upper Nave windows constructed

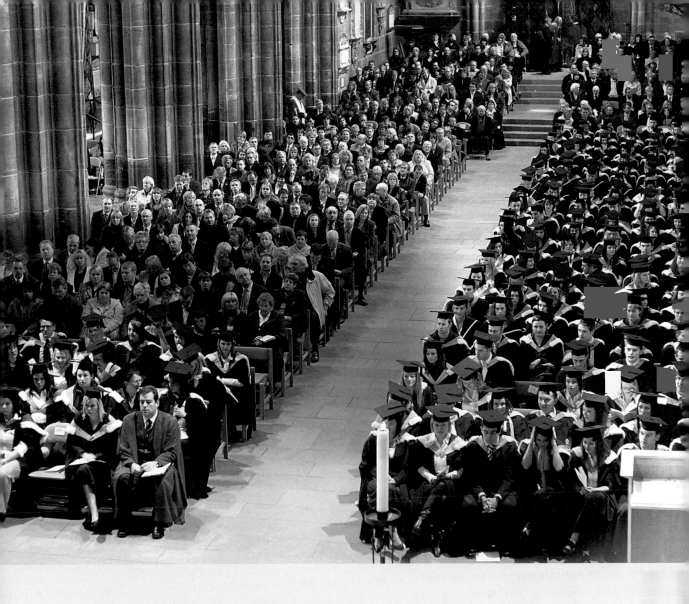

Henry VIII signs
the Letters
Patent creating
the Cathedral,
4th July; church
is made as
usable as
possible

1541

Restoration
work begins

1830s

Large-scale
restoration
under Sir
George
Gilbert Scott

1868–76

South
Transept
ceiling built

1900–02

Stained
glass windows
installed in
the Cloisters

1921–26

West
Window
installed

1961

Westminster
Windows
installed in
the Nave

1992

Song School
completed

2005

1540

Monastery
dissolved,
4th February,
and building
work ceases,
leaving
the church
unfinished

1636

Consistory
Court is
moved from
the Lady
Chapel to the
unfinished
south-west
tower

1835

Stained glass
re-introduced
into the
Cathedral

1880

South
Transept
reabsorbed
into the
Cathedral

1911–13

East, north
and west
Cloisters
restored by
Giles Gilbert
Scott

1939

New Refectory
ceiling

1975

Separate
Bell Tower
opened

1997

New stone
floor and
under-floor
heating in
the Nave

Introduction

C hester Cathedral has had an unusually long and complicated history. The present church was not originally built as a cathedral, a bishop's church, but was founded as a monastery in 1092; monks following the Rule of St Benedict lived, worked and worshipped here for many hundreds of years and have left clear evidence of their way of life. The monastery church in turn succeeded at least two earlier churches on the site, and may even have had a Roman predecessor.

Building work continued off and on throughout the life of the monastery, initially as a Romanesque building, of which some traces remain. The Romanesque church was gradually replaced with one in the later Gothic style, however, beginning with the construction of the Lady Chapel in about 1260.

Further change came in the sixteenth century with the closing of the monastery by Henry VIII in 1540, followed almost immediately, in 1541, by its re-constitution as the cathedral of the new diocese of Chester. Instead of falling into disrepair, the 'old' monastery became the 'new' cathedral; so what we see here today is not only a cathedral but also one of the country's finest examples of a monastic complex, sprawling over a quarter of the area of the medieval settlement.

The North Nave Aisle, showing the Victorian mosaics designed by John Clayton.

History

Roman Chester

Britain became part of the Roman Empire in AD43 but it was only around AD70, under the Emperor Vespasian, that a new policy of total conquest led to a permanent military presence at Chester. Troops stationed here were well placed to deal with two troublesome tribes, the Ordovices to the north and the Brigantes in North Wales. Chester was the highest navigable point on the river Dee and, with its superb harbour, river crossing and readily defensible position, was strategically placed between the two tribes, offering a gateway into both regions and a possible embarkation point for a Roman invasion of Ireland.

By about AD80 the new fortress had already reached its full size; comparable fortresses of the time covered some 50 acres of land but at Chester the enclosure measured just short of 60 acres, implying that the site was particularly important to its Roman builders and may have accommodated a separate naval detachment within the fortress, possibly related to an invasion of Ireland.

The fort was constructed according to the normal pattern of Roman military bases, rectangular in outline, with a gateway in the centre of each side giving access to the major streets. It is reputed that a Roman temple to Apollo was built on the site of the present Cathedral but this is unconfirmed.

Christianity became the state religion of Rome under the Emperor Constantine in the early years of the fourth century and, as a great Roman settlement, it is entirely likely that a church was built in the city, or that the Roman temple was rededicated, thus placing the church on the site of the present Cathedral. The tenth-century Welsh Annals mention a synod at 'Urbs Legionis' (the 'City of the Legions') which was attended by seven British bishops in AD601, and although it is not mentioned by name, Chester seems the most likely place for this meeting.

The fort was still occupied until the late fourth century, but the early fifth century saw the end of the Roman military occupation, although it seems that the old legionary defences continued to be used by a civilian population for security against raiders from the Irish Sea.

Roman remains

The columns above the great Romanesque arch in the North Transept are said to be Roman. The arch was built as part of the Norman church, in around 1100, when Roman remains in the city would still have been very evident. The Norman masons must have decided to re-cycle the columns by using them in their building; in fact, up to 75% of the Romanesque work here is made up of re-cycled Roman building material.

So the arch is almost 1000 years old, but these small columns are nearly 1000 years older still!

The distinctive outline of the Cathedral Tower, rising above the Georgian rooftops of Abbey Street.

Saxon Saint

In the aftermath of the Roman occupation, the country initially split into a number of small states but, by the sixth and seventh centuries, larger and more unified kingdoms began to appear, notably Northumbria in the north and Mercia in the Midlands. It seems that Chester remained a centre of some importance throughout the period, falling under Saxon control during the seventh-century expansion of Mercia. According to Henry Bradshawe, a fifteenth-century chronicler of the life of St Werburgh, the Mercian king Wulfhere (ruled 657–75) founded a church on the cathedral site, dedicated to Saints Peter and Paul, in around 660; this would have been a small timber building, which has completely disappeared.

Wulfhere's daughter, Werburgh, was to prove immensely important in the development of the building. Renouncing her royal status, she became a nun at the abbey in Ely, but was recalled by Wulfhere's successor Aethelred, who made her abbess 'over all the nuns of every monastery within his realm' (Goscelin, 'The Life of St Werburgh', c.1090). She is said to have performed many miracles to alleviate sickness, trouble, pain or personal problems but she was best known for miraculously restoring to life a goose that had been stolen and eaten.

Werburgh died on 3rd February, probably in 706, and her feast day is still observed on this date. Nine years after her death, her nephew Coelred decided to create a more fitting tomb; when the coffin was opened in the presence of the king and his council, the body was said to be 'in whole and perfect form', one of the attributes of a saint. The new tomb very soon became the site of various miracles, inspiring pilgrimage. Many were apparently cured by simply touching the tomb while praying or after drinking the water from the well of the church. Accordingly, Werburgh was acclaimed a saint by popular approval rather than by formal dedication, a common occurrence at that time.

In 875, the tomb was threatened by an invading Danish army and so the relics were brought to safety in the walled city of Chester and deposited in the church of Saints Peter and Paul; from that time onward,

This figure of Saint Werburgh is in the Cloisters.

St Werburgh, shown in the Great West Window of 1961.

21st June has been kept as St Werburgh's 'Festival in the Summer'. Queen Ethelfleda, daughter of King Alfred the Great, decided to found a monastery in Werburgh's name and to rededicate the existing church in her honour. She also refortified the walls of Chester, making it a centre of government by 908. Cheshire was thus Chester's shire, and indeed was often known as Chestershire until the fifteenth century.

The new monastery continued to enjoy royal patronage. A charter of King Edgar in 958 grants land to support a *'familia'* serving 'Almighty God in honour of the most holy Werburgh ever virgin'. The monastery is mentioned in the Domesday Book: 'In the city of Chester the Church of St Werburgh has xiii houses quit of all custom.' Miracles continued to occur, and the relics, held in a reliquary, were carried out of the church onto the walls in order to defend the city, repelling, according to tradition, the armies of 'Griffin', King of Wales, the Danish King Harold and Malcolm II of Scotland.

The fact that the Benedictine monastery built in 1092 was also dedicated to St Werburgh shows that the saint remained a powerful local figure even after the Norman Conquest.

Benedictine Monastery

Chester was the last English city to fall before the Norman conqueror, William I, after two rebellions in the area. He reached Chester in 1070 and met fierce resistance, almost half the houses in the city being destroyed and the surrounding area ravaged mercilessly. In order to bring the area firmly under Norman rule, William appointed his nephew, Hugh d'Avranches, as the first Norman Earl of Chester, and made Cheshire a County Palatine, almost a self-contained city state, with its own law courts and civil service. Earl Hugh was nicknamed *'lupus'* ('the Wolf') which gives some indication of his character.

Having built Chester Castle, Hugh Lupus decided to found a monastery in the heart of his administrative capital and invited Anselm, one of the greatest theologians of his age, to

Medieval shrine

The shrine of St Werburgh that we see today at the west end of the Lady Chapel dates from c.1340 and is a rare survivor from medieval England, since most were destroyed at the Reformation. Originally it would have been surmounted by pinnacles, giving the appearance of a small Chapel inside the larger church. It would have been painted and covered in jewels and other offerings and must have presented a very impressive sight. The upper part of the shrine would have held a reliquary containing the saint's relics; the healing power of the saint was believed to suffuse the stone itself and pilgrims would kneel at the niches in the lower level – some even sat in them in order to get closer, and as a result the niches were sometimes called 'squeezing spaces'.

In 1538, the shrine was dismantled and incorporated into the throne of the first bishop of the newly created diocese of Chester. According to legend, the relics were buried somewhere in the Lady Chapel. The shrine was reconstructed in 1873 by Sir Arthur Blomfield, after several missing pieces were discovered.

The extended South Transept dates from c.1350.

The Romanesque arch in the North Transept dates from the foundation of the monastery in 1092.

supervise the transformation of the Saxon church into a large and well-endowed Benedictine monastery. Anselm's clerk, Richard, became the first abbot (he died in 1133 and his coffin can now be seen in the South Cloister walk), and the original monks almost certainly came from the great French abbey of Bec.

Hugh Lupus's church was built in the style known as 'Romanesque', so-called because it was inspired by the round arches and massive columns of ancient Roman buildings. The Nave was approximately the same size as we see today; the present Baptistery forms the base of a Norman north-west tower, indicating the westerly extent of the church. The north wall of the Nave (under the mosaics) is also part of the Norman church; on the Cloister side of this wall, round arches can still be seen. The east end was probably semi-circular, with the High Altar in the centre and the shrine of St Werburgh standing behind it. This layout is typical of church design of the period and can be seen in many other locations, such as Canterbury Cathedral and Westminster Abbey.

Originally the South Transept (one 'arm' of the cross shape of the church) was the same size as the North, but it was enlarged in later years and it is in the North Transept that we get our best idea of the appearance of the Norman church. It was not as high as the present building; the gallery that can be seen today is probably an indication of the original height. And it must have been very dark; just beneath the gallery in the wall opposite the great arch you will see three small openings (now blocked up) which were the original windows. This lack of light was

Left: The north walk of the Cloisters, showing the *lavatorium*, or monks' washplace, on the left and the arch to the Day Stairs at the far end.

quite intentional; the monks were trying to create a 'mysterious' atmosphere in the original sense of the word, to emphasise the 'mystery' of God. Just for a second, imagine yourself in a very dark and atmospheric building, the monks chanting in the background, candles flickering in the gloom catching the glint of gold from icons on the walls and clouds of incense blowing about; you will soon get some conception of the atmosphere in the great church.

The Chapter House, showing the magnificent Victorian stained glass window.

Building began in 1092 at the East End, which was the most important part to the monks since the services took place here. Once this was well advanced, attention was turned to the domestic buildings, including the Cloisters and rooms such as the Undercroft and the Refectory which opened off the central square. The Chapter House was the last part of the domestic buildings to be completed, c.1250, in the recently introduced Gothic style, with pointed arches and ribbed vaults. The Norman church, with its round-headed arches, must have looked very old-fashioned by comparison, and it seems that the monks decided to rebuild their church in the new style, beginning c.1270 at the East End with the construction of a new Lady Chapel.

The construction of the new church continued with the remodelling of the Quire in 1290, the Crossing in about 1300 and the South Transept in 1350. The south side of the Nave was rebuilt in 1360, the north side not until 1490; this long break in building was apparently caused by labour shortages resulting from successive waves of plague.

Building carried on into the sixteenth century; the West End was constructed about 1515/20 and work then moved aloft, to construct the upper windows and stone ceilings. Henry VIII's reformation of the English Church intervened, however, and the monastery was dissolved in 1539. Consequently, the builders erected plain wooden ceilings over the church, rather than the elaborate stone vaults which they had intended.

Cathedral Church

The monastery of St Werburgh suffered less destruction than most religious houses at the Reformation, owing to Henry's decision in 1541 to subdivide the huge diocese of Lichfield, which stretched from south of Coventry to the Scottish borders, and to create a new diocese of Chester. This new diocese needed a cathedral for its bishop and, rather than build a new cathedral, it was decided to re-use the old monastery church, which had been surrendered by the last abbot, John Clarke, on 20th January 1540.

Building work ceased at that time but it was known that the old monastery would become the new cathedral and so the unfinished building was hurriedly patched up to allow services to continue inside. The following year, 26th July 1541, by order of King Henry VIII, the monastery church was reconstituted as 'the Cathedral Church of Christ and the Blessed Virgin Mary in Chester'.

The parishioners of the collegiate church of St Oswald had been granted the right to worship in the South Transept of the monastery church when their parish church had been merged with the monastery in 1093. In the thirteenth century the monks built a separate church for them, opposite the monastery, but towards the end of the fifteenth century they successfully reclaimed the South Transept as their parish church. Great wooden screens were erected to separate it from the main body of the church, remaining in place until 1880, when the South Transept was at last reunited with the Cathedral.

A master mason carved high in the Quire.

Like most religious foundations, Chester suffered damage during the Civil War and the Commonwealth period in the seventeenth century. All the medieval stained glass windows were smashed and replaced with plain glass because they were thought to be idolatrous; it was not until 1835 that coloured glass was re-introduced to the Cathedral. A visible reminder of this destruction is the memorial to Thomas Greene in the South Transept, where the three figures' hands have been destroyed because they were joined in prayer, regarded at the time as a popish gesture.

A memorial from 1602 to Thomas Greene and both his wives; the praying hands were chopped off during the Civil War in the mid-seventeenth century.

By the nineteenth century, it was clear that the building needed restoration. Some work was undertaken in the 1830s but the major restoration took place 1868–76 under the supervision of noted Victorian architect and church restorer Sir George Gilbert Scott. Further large-scale restoration continued for many years; later work includes the opening up of the north-west tower as a Baptistery by Sir Arthur Blomfield in 1885 and the installation in 1883–86 of the Nave mosaics designed by John Clayton. One major undertaking was the re-roofing of the South Transept in 1900–02, designed by Charles James Blomfield, Sir Arthur Blomfield's son. The Cloisters and Refectory were restored 1911–13 by Giles Gilbert Scott, who also worked on the restoration of the Refectory in 1914. The Cloisters were glazed 1921–26, and a new ceiling was installed in the Refectory in 1939.

The Great West Window dates from 1961 and replaces a Victorian window which was blown out by a bomb in 1941, thankfully the only major damage inflicted on the Cathedral in World War II. The external Bell Tower was opened in 1975, the stone floor of the Nave dates from 1997 and the Song School was completed in 2005.

Thus each part of the building represents the work of many generations, combining to make the Cathedral that we see today.

The figure of King David holding his harp, from the mosaics of 1883–86 which decorate the north wall of the Nave.

Chester Cathedral Today

The thirteenth-century Abbey Gateway leads into Abbey Square. The large arch was for carts, while the smaller arch provided pedestrian access.

Abbey Square

This charming square originally formed part of the abbey precinct and was called the 'Great Court'. Around it were grouped domestic buildings including the brewhouse, bake-house, kitchens and stables. It was redeveloped in the eighteenth and early nineteenth centuries with new residences for genteel families but a number of older buildings can still be seen, notably the Abbey Gateway on the west side, probably built around 1350. This was the 'front line' between monastery and city; through it would have come an endless stream of deliveries and tradesmen, as well as pilgrims and those seeking the hospitality

Right: The Nave, North Transept and Tower of the Cathedral rise over the roof of the Cloisters.

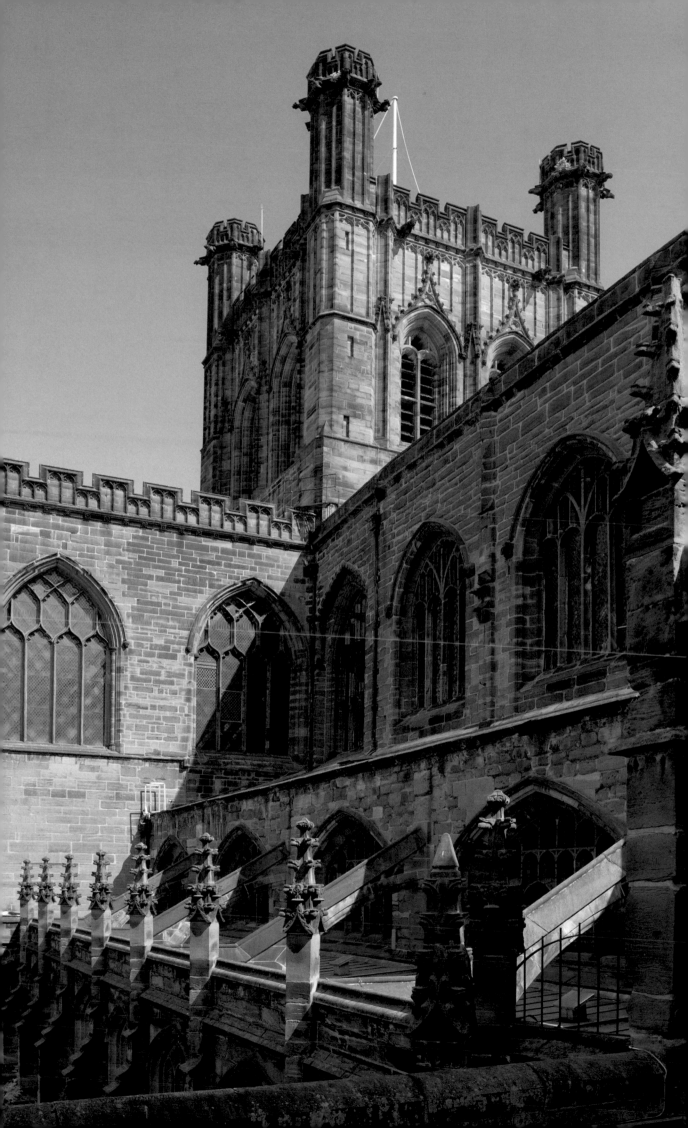

Disraeli defending Crown and Country.

This scene represents Gladstone's 'Vatican Pamphlets' of 1874.

Font

The font is Italian and was given to the Cathedral by a local aristocrat, Earl Egerton of Tatton Park, near Knutsford, who believed it was an Etruscan well-head dating from the seventh-century BC; however, it is now thought to be a nineteenth-century reproduction of earlier work. The peacocks carved on the side are an early Christian symbol of the new and eternal life given to believers when they are baptised.

and protection of the monastery. The upper storey is an eighteenth-century addition, part of the Georgian redevelopment. Notice the stone 'wheelers' laid in the cobbles of the square in order to provide a smooth ride for coaches and carriages.

Leading off the square is Abbey Street, an elegant terrace of eighteenth-century houses facing the Cathedral; the street leads to the Kaleyard Gate beyond which was the monastery's vegetable patch. In order to create a shortcut to the plot, the abbot requested permission to make a doorway through the city wall in 1275; this was granted, with the condition that the monks were responsible for its security.

The Cathedral Exterior

The outside of the building was refaced as part of the Victorian restoration of 1868–76 and so does not fully reflect the medieval interior. The Tower dates from the late fifteenth century. Its outer shell has been much altered, particularly by the addition of four corner turrets, part of Sir George Gilbert Scott's uncompleted plan for a great spire on top of the tower. Perhaps the most unusual aspect of the exterior is the conical roof at the east end of the South Quire Aisle. Sir George Gilbert Scott shortened the aisle considerably, returning it to its thirteenth-century dimensions and adding this curious feature, for which he apparently found irrefutable evidence!

Nearby can be seen the Bell Tower, designed by George Pace and opened in 1975, the first free-standing bell tower built for a cathedral since the fifteenth century. By the late 1960s, it was clear that the bells themselves were placing great stress on the medieval tower and a separate tower was seen as the most appropriate solution.

Tucked away on the exterior, in the angle of the south-east corner of the South Transept, are stone portraits of the two leading nineteenth-century politicians, Gladstone and Disraeli. On the right, Gladstone, with a pen in his mouth, seems to be attacking the Roman Catholic Church, represented by a cardinal and the papal tiara; on the left, Disraeli can be seen defending the Crown with a sword.

The Baptistery, showing masonry of the twelfth century and a seventeenth-century lantern.

Baptistery

Entering the Cathedral from the South Cloister, the visitor is at once in one of the oldest parts. To the right of the entrance, in the north-west corner of the Nave, is the Baptistery, forming the base of one of the two towers which flanked the West End of the Romanesque church. The sixteenth-century plan was to rebuild these towers but work only proceeded as far as the lower level of the south-east tower on the opposite side, which now contains the Consistory Court. As a result, masonry dating from about 1140 can still be seen in this part of the Cathedral.

After the Reformation, the north-west tower was divided by an additional floor and was walled off from the rest of the church; the Baptistery as we see it today was created in 1885, by Sir Arthur Blomfield. The mosaic pavement illustrates baptism and confirmation; it was designed by Revd. John Howson (Dean of Chester 1867–85) and awaits restoration.

On the plinth of the twelfth-century north-east column, a game of Nine Men's Morris can be seen scratched into the stone; this is similar to the modern game of Ludo and was perhaps carved by a bored monk to pass the time!

Consistory Court

The room at the base of the unfinished south-west tower forms a fascinating and unique survival: the only old church court, or Consistory Court, in this country. Initially sited in the Lady Chapel, it was moved to its present location in 1636, a date recorded on the typically Renaissance screen over the door.

The great table is believed to date from c.1600 and the canopy over the raised seat has been altered to fit, losing part of the name of Edward Mainwaring, Chancellor of the diocese in 1634. The arms of the see of Chester (three mitres) can also be seen, with the wolf's head badge of Hugh Lupus.

The Consistory Court is unique, since it is the only old church court in the country. The woodwork dates from the late sixteenth century and was moved to its present location in 1636.

The court dealt with the legal work of the diocese, including handling wills and probate and fining those who failed to attend their parish churches or misbehaved during services. The court was essentially a postal operation, handling a vast amount of correspondence. This explains both the enormous size of the table and the raised seat in the corner, enabling the apparitor (who was responsible for the smooth running of the operation) literally to oversee proceedings. The chancellor himself sat in the raised and canopied seat, with a clerk on either side.

The Gothic building plan envisaged two great towers soaring up on either side of the West Front, but the builders only constructed the first stage on the south-west side; this was built around 1508, by Abbot Birchenshaw (1493–1537), and the unfinished shafts and bare masonry in the corners of the room show that vaulting was intended.

The Nave, looking towards the West Window of 1961; worship regularly takes place in this area.

Nave

The Nave is the largest part of the Cathedral and was the last area to be rebuilt. The arches on the south side were begun in about 1360, but those on the north were not completed until 1490, a break of some 130 years. The reason for this break is the Black Death, the plague that swept the country in the mid-fourteenth century, which killed between a third and a half of the population; there were simply not enough workers available. By the time the arches on the north side were built, the prevailing architectural style had changed to the Perpendicular and arches were becoming rather flatter and less pointed. Here, however, the two sides of the Nave are almost identical – clearly the architect of the north side has copied the design on the south. This conscious copying of an earlier style is very rare, appearing on this scale at only two other places in the country, Westminster Abbey in London and Beverley Minster in east Yorkshire.

The West End was completed around 1515/20 and the monastery was dissolved before the upper windows could be completed or the Nave vaulted with a ribbed stone ceiling. Some sort of temporary wooden roof must have been put up in order for services to take place in the newly constituted Cathedral. The present ceiling was constructed during the Victorian restoration of 1868–76, of wood in order not to overload the medieval walls. The designer was Sir George Gilbert Scott, who wrote in 1870:

> 'Among our greatest internal works will be the completion of the vaulting – the aisles in stone, but the higher vaults in oak – as we fear to load the pillars and clerestory walls with stone. That of the Nave is now in preparation. It follows precisely the lines given by the incipient ribs contained in the old stone springers. I have taken the vaulting of the beautiful neighbouring chancel at Nantwich for my guide as to the more ornamental portions.'

The ceiling was cleaned, the oak ribs were limed and the carved wooden ceiling bosses gilded in 1997.

Chester Imp

This carved representation of the Devil in chains is set high up in the clerestory windows of the Nave, in the second window from the east on the north side. The story is that a monk walking along the gallery saw the Devil looking in the window and in a panic told the abbot. The abbot had the carving made to warn the Devil of what would happen if he dared to return.

It is significant that the carving is on the north side of the building. In medieval times evil spirits were believed to come from the north, presumably because it is cold and damp, and images of chained devils were intended to frighten these evil spirits away. Whatever the stories, the Imp seems to have worked. There have been no further reports of the Devil looking in the window!

The great mosaics on the north wall are also Victorian work, dating from 1883–86, and show four characters from the Old Testament: Abraham, Moses, David and Elijah. They were designed by John Clayton and executed by Burke & Co. They represent one of the largest examples of Pre-Raphaelite mosaic work in an English Cathedral and are true mosaics, in that they are made of different shades of marble rather than ceramic tiles.

The modern windows on the south side of the Nave were donated in 1992 by the present Duke of Westminster, in memory of his parents and to commemorate the 900th anniversary of

The head of the young David, from the mosaics in the north Nave.

the founding of the monastery. They were designed by Alan Younger and incorporate the themes of continuity and change. In the window tracery can be seen Victorian angels which survived the bomb of 1941 and which have been incorporated in the later design.

The sandstone floor of the Nave was re-laid in 1997; the old floor had been laid in 1776, using extremely low grade sandstone, and by the 1990s was in very poor condition, having been badly repaired over the years. Under-floor heating was installed at the same time, which has made a great difference to the winter temperature of the Cathedral! The four splendid cast iron stoves by the London Heating and Ventilation Company, which used to heat the building, have been left in place as a remembrance of times past.

At the west end of the Nave, a flight of steps leads up to the west doors, which are opened only on ceremonial occasions. The colourful curtains over the door date from 1997 and are designed to reflect the colours of the Great West Window above. The Cathedral is built on rock which slopes upwards to the west and the steps follow its line. At the top of the steps stands a black marble font, which was given to the Cathedral in 1687 by William Morton, Bishop, first, of Kildare and then of Meath.

The dominant feature of the Nave, however, is surely the Great West Window, which dates from 1961. Designed by W.T. Carter Shapland, it shows the Holy Family in the two central lights, surrounded by the northern saints Werburgh (far left), Oswald, Aidan, Chad, Wilfred and Queen Ethelfleda. Interestingly, the inspiration of the window is medieval, with individual figures in each light, a scene from their lives below (the exception is Adam and Eve beneath the Blessed Virgin), and symbolism and imagery above, the most obvious example being the three rings of the Trinity at the top of the window. The colour of the glass looks back to the jewel-like colours of early medieval glass, which was also very popular in the early 1960s; a similar use of colour can be seen in the windows of the modern Cathedral at Coventry, dating from the same period.

Great West Window.

The South Transept was built in the thirteenth century to accommodate these four extra chapels; the stained glass windows are Victorian.

South Transept

The rebuilding of the South Transept was probably begun in about 1350 by Abbot Richard de Seynesbury (1349–63) but the work took a long time and the enlargement of the Transept, to accommodate four extra chapels for the singing of daily Masses, caused something of a problem. In the standard medieval plan, two chapels would be placed on either side of the church, in transepts of equal size, thus maintaining the traditional cross-shaped design. The Vestibule and Chapter House already lay to the north, however, and there was no room to expand further. The four extra chapels were therefore all placed on the south side, forming the huge transept that we see today.

By the time the chapels were built, Gothic architecture had entered the next stage of its development, the 'Decorated' phase. This can be seen most clearly in the design of the windows; the tracery in the tops of the windows is much more elaborate than that in the earlier Lady Chapel. The oak ceiling over the main part of the transept dates from the restoration of 1900–02 and was designed by C.J. Blomfield; the only medieval vault in the transept is that above the Chapel of Saints Nicholas and Leonard.

The first of the four chapels (nearest to the Crossing) is dedicated to St Mary Magdalene and the Ascension and is now used as the Children's Chapel; the reredos behind the altar was designed in 1922 by Charles Tower, in memory of John Darby, Dean of Chester (1886–1919), and the window, designed by Heaton, Butler & Bayne, dates from 1876. The next chapel is dedicated to St Oswald. The reredos (which was carved in Oberammergau by Johannes Zwinck) and the stained glass window were designed by Charles Kempe, one of the best known

The Chapel of St George is dedicated to the 22nd Cheshire Regiment, which was founded in 1689 and now forms part of the 1st Battalion the Mercian Regiment (Cheshires).

Above: A detail of St George slaying the dragon, from the carving in the Chapel of St George. This dates from 1921 and was designed by Sir Giles Gilbert Scott.

Below: A memorial to Hugh Lupus Grosvenor (1825–99); created the first Duke of Westminster in 1874, he was MP for Chester for 22 years from 1847–69.

D·IN·MEMORY·OF·HUGH·LUPUS·GROSVENOR·F

stained glass designers of the nineteenth century. The third chapel is dedicated to St George; again the stained glass is by Charles Kempe, while the reredos of St George and the dragon was designed by Sir Giles Gilbert Scott in 1921. The final chapel is dedicated to Saints Nicholas and Leonard; the stained glass window by Clayton & Bell dates from 1880, while the reredos was designed by Sir Giles Gilbert Scott in 1917.

The enormous stained glass window at the far end of the Transept dates from 1887; it was designed by Heaton, Butler & Bayne in 1886 and represents 'The Triumph of Faith'. The window was erected in memory of Lord Egerton of Tatton and the design was later exhibited at the Royal Academy in 1888.

On the west side of the Transept stands a fine memorial to Hugh Lupus Grosvenor, the first Duke of Westminster (1825–99), in whose memory the South Transept was restored. The memorial dates from 1902 and was designed by Charles James Blomfield; the marble effigy was carved by F.W. Pomeroy and this design was also exhibited at the Royal Academy, in 1901.

There are a number of military memorials in the South Transept, including various colours of the Cheshire Regiment and the Regimental Rolls of Honour of the First and Second World Wars. One memorial of particular note is that to Jack Cornwell, the youngest recipient of the Victoria Cross in the World War I, who served on HMS Chester and lost his life at the Battle of Jutland. The citation from his commanding officer, Admiral Beatty, describes how he 'was mortally wounded early in the action, but nevertheless remained standing alone at a most exposed post, quietly awaiting orders till the end of the action, with the gun's crew dead and wounded around him.' The Cornwell medal is still the highest award in scouting.

Above the Cornwell Memorial is a plaque to Frederick Philips, a reminder of Chester's many links with the United States. Philips, born in 1720 in 'the province of New York', 'opposed at the hazard of his life, the late rebellion in North America' (the American War of Independence) and 'his estate, one of the largest in New York, was confiscated by the

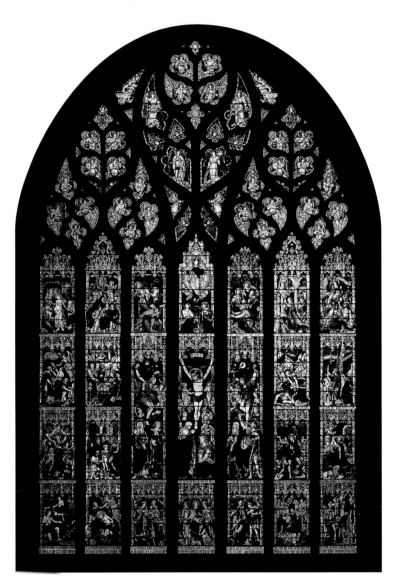

South window.

usurped legislature of that Province'. He came over to England a rather poorer man and died in 1785. His house, Philipsburg Manor, is an American National Historic Landmark, while the church built by the Philips family in Sleepy Hollow was the inspiration for Washington Irving's famous ghost story.

Crossing

The Crossing lies at the heart of the Cathedral, with the Tower above it stretching high over the city skyline. It was begun around 1300 but not finished until about 150 years later. The Tower is supported by two great intersecting arches called the 'Crown of Stone', a unique method of bearing the weight above. The cathedral bells hung in the Tower until the late 1960s, when the Tower was found to be cracking, and so a free-standing Bell Tower, designed by George Pace, was built to the south-west of the Cathedral.

Nineteenth-century restoration work is particularly evident here; the wooden screen which separates the Quire from the Nave was constructed in 1876 to designs by Sir George Gilbert Scott, intended to harmonise with the fourteenth-century wood carving in the Quire. The wooden screen replaced a solid stone one which originally separated the monastic part of the building from the rest of the church. Scott wanted to follow Victorian liturgy and open up the view of the High Altar from the Nave, however, and so he moved the stone screen to a position behind the Quire stalls (it can still be seen above the medieval tiles in the North Quire Aisle) and replaced it with the open wooden screen we see today. The centrepiece of Christ on the cross flanked by Mary and John, which dates from 1913, was designed by Sir Giles Gilbert Scott, Sir George's grandson, and carved by Ferdinand Stuflesser, a craftsman from the Austrian Tyrol. George Gilbert Scott also designed the intricate mosaic floor which dates from 1875. The red and gold decoration on the ceiling was designed by George Pace in 1969; above it is the floor of the old bell-ringing chamber.

The organ loft was donated by the first Duke of Westminster in 1876 and several coats of arms relating to the family can be seen on the gallery and under the loft. The Duke of Westminster's family seat, Eaton Hall, is just outside Chester, and the family have been great benefactors of the Cathedral for many years. A very beautiful fifteenth-century sculpture in low relief of the Madonna and Child was placed here as a memorial to Lady Sibell Mary, Countess Grosvenor, who died in 1929. The columns supporting the loft appear to be marble but in fact they are hollow, with supporting iron girders running up inside. They are made of *scagliola*, a mixture of fine plaster of powdered selenite (gypsum), alum, glue, water, and pigment, which creates the appearance of marble; the colouring was created by the use of blackberry juice!

On the south-west side of the Crossing is a Tudor memorial to Thomas Greene, Sheriff of Chester in 1551 and Mayor in 1565. He is shown as the central figure, with his two wives on either side of him. Originally the figures had 'praying hands' but, during the Civil War of the mid-seventeenth century, extreme Protestants, regarding such hands as Catholic and idolatrous, chopped them off.

The organ

To the north, the organ towers over the Crossing. The present instrument was placed here by Sir George Gilbert Scott in 1876 but incorporates pipes from the previous organ of 1844, which stood on the stone screen, obstructing the view into the Quire. This was removed by Scott to open up the view from the Nave. He also designed the new organ case (1875–76). There was not enough room for all the pipes required, however, and so the organ, which is played from the manuals in the loft above, is split into three sections; the bass pipes can be seen in the North Transept and the choir organ lies behind the stalls on the south side of the Quire. In all, there are 4864 pipes.

Rushworth & Dreaper of Liverpool overhauled the instrument in 1969, providing a new mechanism and some new pipework, notably flute mutations on the solo organ and extra mixtures on each division. This added significantly to the tonal palette available for effective performance of baroque and modern music.

The impressive inlaid floor of the Crossing was designed by Sir George Gilbert Scott and made by John Thomson & Sons in 1875-76.

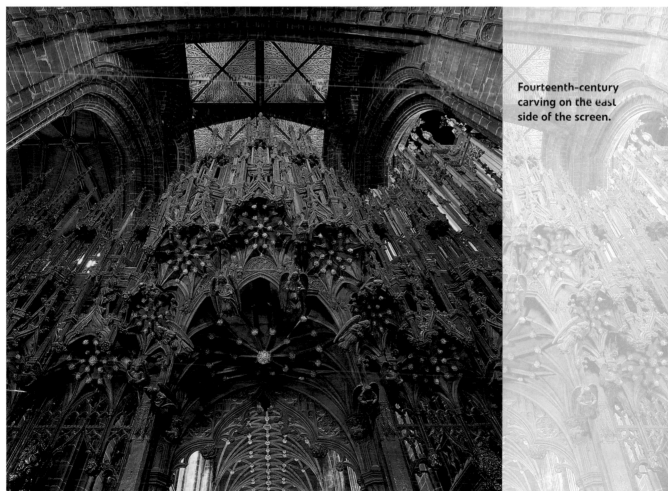

Fourteenth-century carving on the east side of the screen.

The builders

Quire

Building work on the Quire began about 1280, immediately after the Lady Chapel, as the next part of the east to west rebuilding process, and in a rather more decorated, late thirteenth-century Gothic style. It has a typical three-storey design: arches, then a triforium (the row of smaller arches), followed by a clerestory (or 'clear story') to light the interior of the church. There are puzzles, however. The triforium of the two eastern bays on the north side differs from the rest and was probably built slightly earlier. The design of the columns also varies considerably.

It seems that the design varies so much because at least six master masons worked on the Quire. Chester was the gathering point for the Welsh campaigns waged by Edward I, who also built several castles in North Wales; where better to look for master masons than a half-built church? In return Edward sent one of his chief masons to Chester, Richard L'Enginour (or 'engineer'); stonework in the Quire has echoes at Caernarvon Castle, where Richard also worked. He later settled in Chester.

The High Altar dates from the nineteenth-century restoration and lies rather further to

The High Altar.

Right: The Quire and High Altar.

A fragment of medieval glass, showing a resurrected figure.

The figure of Judas Iscariot in the High Altar mosaic; note the absence of a halo.

The fourteenth-century seats or *sedilia*, for the officiating clergy.

the east than the medieval altar. It is usually covered by a rich frontal in one of the symbolic colours of the Church's year, white at Christmas and Easter or purple in Lent and Advent. The floor tiles of the Quire are similar to those in the Lady Chapel and again date from the Victorian restoration of 1868–76; the frames of the pictures in the pavement of the Sanctuary are formed of small squares of stone (called '*tesserae*') from the site of the Temple of Jerusalem. The stained glass in the East Window (over the altar) shows the Presentation of Christ in the Temple; it dates from 1884 and was designed by Heaton, Butler & Bayne. The large bronze candelabra, which were originally in the church of St Tomaso in Milan, were made by Orazio Censorio (died 1622), an iron maker from Rome who held the unusual title of 'cannon-maker to the Pope'.

The mosaic behind the altar dates from about 1880 and was designed by Clayton & Bell and made by Venetian mosaicist Antonio Salviati, who developed a process of sandwiching a layer of gold between two layers of glass, resulting in the exceptionally rich decoration seen here. To the right of the altar the *sedilia*, seats provided for the clergy,

The intricate carving of the monastic Quire stalls.

date from the fourteenth century. The bishop's throne (*cathedra* in both Latin and Greek, the building in which a bishop presides taking its name from his chair) is nineteenth-century but was carved in sympathy with the magnificent Quire stalls which date from 1380. The splendid ceiling, showing the angelic orchestra and Old Testament prophets, also dates from about 1875/80 and was designed by J.R. Clayton.

The great treasure of Chester Cathedral, however, is the carved oak woodwork of the seats or Quire stalls. These were probably constructed c.1380, almost certainly by the same craftsmen who made the stalls in Lincoln Cathedral ten years earlier, as the two sets of stalls are clearly related. They show the influence of the King's master carpenters, a father and son team, William and Hugh Herland, who later built the great hammer beam roof of Westminster Hall.

It was in the Quire that the monks sang their Daily Offices, known as *opus dei* (the work of God); there were seven services and two masses each day, starting at about midnight with Matins and Lauds. The Rule of St. Benedict required the monks to sing the Daily Offices standing up, with the hinged seat of the stall upright. As early as the twelfth century, mention is made of small ledges attached to the underneath of seats, allowing the monks to rest; these are termed misericords, from the Latin *misericordia*, pity. Craftsmen were quick to realise the decorative potential of these ledges, particularly as they were relatively inaccessible; apprentices could try out their skills and master craftsmen could indulge their imaginations and sense of humour.

One of the carved misericords which allowed a monk to rest his legs.

The delightful, quirky carvings that resulted are not simply charming scenes of medieval life – although that element is certainly present. To the medieval mind, every aspect of earthly existence was interpreted as representing a manifestation of God's will and so the carvings take on a deeper significance. Subjects are taken from legend, the lives of the saints and everyday life; probably the most important source was the *Bestiary*, a book which blended (often wildly misinterpreted) observations of animal characteristics and behaviour with much misinformation and allegory. Religious scenes are relatively rare – possibly it was considered disrespectful to sit on a representation of the divine! In fact out of the 48 misericords here, only five depict religious scenes.

A carving of a 'Green Man' with acorns and oak leaves.

The Elephant and Castle

This bench-end probably reflects a story from the Crusades, of soldiers on the backs of elephants. But the howdah, the canopied seat, has become a castle, complete with battlements and portcullis! Clearly, the carver had never seen an elephant, as he has given it horse's hooves. Symbolically, it represents the Church bearing the world upon its back.

The tabernacles or canopies above the stalls both sheltered the monks against cold air from the unglazed clerestory windows and improved the acoustics, acting as a form of sounding board. Here again the medieval craftsmen could not resist the opportunity for decoration, and the tabernacles are wonderfully diverse in their design. It is unlikely that the niches were intended to hold statues; the plainer area is supposed to contrast with the decorated surfaces, thus emphasising their ornamentation. Originally, the tabernacles were supported by slender columns rising from the armrests of the back row of the stalls, but these were unaccountably done away with in 1876 and replaced with the carved angels.

In the eighteenth century an attempt was made to 'classicise' the Quire and galleries and Georgian box pews were built. These were removed during Scott's nineteenth-century restoration and extra pews and desk fronts were added, requiring the carving of several new bench-ends. These are rather crisper in execution and slightly paler in colour than the medieval bench-ends, which were given new bases to raise them to the level that the new plan required.

South Quire Aisle

To the right of the High Altar, in the South Quire Aisle, is the Chapel of St Erasmus, dedicated to one of the patron saints of sailors (also known as Elmo) and set aside for private prayer. It holds the tomb of Ranulph Higden, who became a monk here in 1299 and was the author of one of the best-known books of the Middle Ages, the *Polychronicon* (literally 'many stories'), a universal history of the world from the Creation until 1344. Higden is traditionally recognised as the author of the Chester cycle of mystery plays, telling the story of mankind from the Creation to the Last Judgement. The painted ceiling over the altar and the stained glass in the windows form a coherent symbolic scheme designed by Clayton & Bell, representing Faith, Hope, Charity, Humility and Patience. To one side of the altar is a memorial bust of local man Thomas Brassey, one of the great railway builders of the nineteenth century, who built Chester Railway Station in 1847.

The Chapel of St Erasmus.

North Quire Aisle

At the east end of the North Quire Aisle is a chapel dedicated to St Werburgh. The altar here is said to have been made from a fourteenth-century wooden screen, while the wonderful stained glass window in the east wall, representing the Nativity, dates from 1857 and was designed by Arthur and Michael O'Connor. The fine statue of Mary and the young Jesus, taking his first steps, is the work of Harold Gosney and dates from 1999.

Further down the Aisle is a lower area of floor; this is the original floor level of the Norman church. To the left is the base of a circular Romanesque column and on the other side is a column capital which has been incorporated upside down into the foundations of the later building. Also here are some medieval tiles which were found in other parts of the building and placed here for safe keeping. Above the tiles is part of the medieval stone screen that originally ran across the Nave, excluding the monastic parts of the church from public view.

The magnificent iron gates were designed by Alonso Berruguete (1486–1561) and came from Guadalajara in Spain; they were given to the Cathedral in the nineteenth century by the first Duke of Westminster.

Lady Chapel

At the east end of the church is the Lady Chapel, dedicated to the Blessed Virgin Mary. It was built around 1270 and extended east beyond the end of the original Norman church. The cult of the Virgin was at its height and many 'lady' chapels were added to churches at this time. The design of the Chapel is typical Early English Gothic, with tall, thin, 'lancet' windows, intersecting ribs forming the stone ceiling, and three decorative carved bosses covering up the intersections. The first, over the altar, represents the Trinity; the central one shows the Virgin and Child, with angels swinging censers on either side; the third, over the shrine, shows the murder of Thomas á Becket in 1170 in Canterbury Cathedral. One of the relics held by the monastery in the Middle Ages is said to have been the belt of St Thomas, and the monks of Chester were probably trying to associate themselves with the country's greatest martyr cult in order to promote pilgrimage.

The decorative carved boss showing the murder of Thomas à Becket – a rare subject, since Henry VIII ordered the destruction of all such images.

Left: The Chapel of St Werburgh.

The east end of the Lady Chapel.

Two carved heads, possibly representing Abbot Simon de Whitchurch (left), who rebuilt the Lady Chapel, and his prior (right).

Another unexpected feature in the Lady Chapel is the colour on the walls; reconstructed in 1969, this colour scheme reminds us just how brightly decorated medieval churches would have been, with figures of saints painted on the ceiling and perhaps floral decoration on the walls. The floor tiles and stained glass, also part of the nineteenth-century restoration, follow medieval designs. The glass was planned by Dean Howson, as a course of biblical instruction on the Acts of the Apostles, and designed by William Wailes of Newcastle.

At the west end of the Chapel is the shrine of St Werburgh, dating from around 1340 and one of the few such shrines to survive. It formed a suitably rich and elaborate housing for the Saint's relics, which would have been kept in a reliquary in the upper part of the shrine, where the modern statue now stands.

North Transept

Here we see the oldest part of the building still standing today; the great Romanesque (Norman) arch dates back to the foundation of the monastery in 1092. To its right, in a strange juxtaposition, is a Gothic arch, added at the beginning of the fourteenth century. The walls of the Transept were heightened during the fifteenth century and the splendid timber camber beam roof was constructed between 1516 and 1524; it features a number of heraldic badges, including the Tudor rose, and is the oldest wooden ceiling in the Cathedral. It was restored in 1927, and cleaned and decorated in 1969.

Tucked into the corner of the lower part of the shrine of St Werburgh is a tiny carving of a dog, scratching his ear with his back leg. The medieval stonemason is reminding us that everything in the world belongs to God and therefore everything has a place in His church – even a little dog and his fleas!

The gilded and decorated camber beam ceiling of the North Transept dates from the sixteenth century.

Cobweb picture

Beside the great Romanesque arch, in a small niche, is the famous Cobweb picture, showing the Virgin and Child. It is painted onto the net of a caterpillar, a form of craft practised particularly in the Tyrol. This example, one of only 64 in existence, probably dates from the nineteenth century and is a copy of a painting by Lucas Cranach the Elder in the Dom St Jakob, Innsbruck, Austria.

In the centre of the Transept lies the tomb of influential churchman John Pearson, Bishop of Chester 1672–86, who was originally buried near the High Altar. The present tomb dates from 1863 and was designed by Sir Arthur Blomfield. On the west wall is a memorial to the Chester-born artist Randolph Caldecott (1846–86), who greatly influenced the illustration of children's books during the later nineteenth century.

Cloisters

The Cloisters formed the monks' domestic buildings. Around the four sides of the square was everything that was required for day-to-day life and it is here that we can gain the best impression of life in the medieval monastery. Unusually, the Cloisters here are on the north side; owing to the expansion of the city, there was not enough room on the warmer and sunnier south. The south range, forming one wall of the church, has Romanesque round-headed arches and is therefore the earliest surviving part of the Cloister.

The garden, or garth, in the centre was practical rather than decorative. Herbs were particularly important, being used for

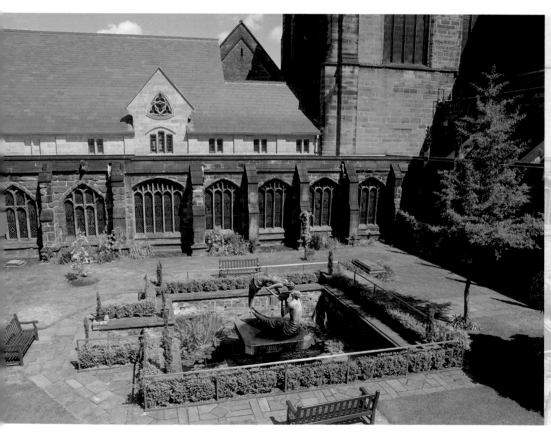

The peaceful cloister gardens; the Song School (opened in 2005) lies on the site of the monastic dormitory.

The *scriptorium* or writing place; the monks' desks were placed here, in the once unglazed Cloisters.

medical purposes as well as cooking, and the pond in the centre was a fish pond. The water was piped in from Abbott's Well, some two miles outside the city; this remarkable feat of engineering dates from 1283, when the spring was given to the monastery by Philip Burnel and his wife, Isabel. The world famous statue, *The Water of Life*, was designed by Steven Broadbent and installed in 1994. It depicts Jesus offering the water of life to the woman of Samaria, a story from the Gospel of St John.

The South Cloister (adjacent to the church) formed the *scriptorium*, where manuscripts were written. In between each of the columns was a desk, sideways on to the window to take advantage of the light; here the monks copied bibles and prayer books and also works of philosophy, history, medicine and even drama – the Chester mystery plays are said to have been written here in the fourteenth century. The stained glass in the windows is modern, dating from the 1920s and 30s; in medieval times these windows were unglazed and there are stories of the monks breaking the ice on top of their inkwells before they began work in the morning! The roof on this side of the Cloister was restored by Sir Giles Gilbert

A memorial to the Cheshire mountaineers, Mallory and Irvine. This small pane of glass is situated to the right of the entrance to the cloister garden.

Scott in 1911–13. The modern stained glass was designed by F.C. Eden and Archibald Nicholson; it represents a calendar of the Church's year and includes figures commemorated in the Church of England.

At the top of the West Cloister is a curious doorway with a column in front of it. The door led to the abbot's private lodgings up above and dates from about 1135; but the column in front of it was added as a roofing support in 1527–29, when the stone ceiling replaced an earlier wooden one. Each side of the Cloister was subdivided into ten equal spaces and the roofing supports were inserted regardless of what was already there. It is interesting that such a major building project was carried out in a time of religious upheaval.

The west side of the Cloister, which now houses the Visitors' Entrance and the Cathedral Shop, would originally have been the cellar of the monastery, where all the provisions were stored. The squat solid columns and the simple groin vaulting date from approximately 1140 and are typical of the Romanesque period.

Monks' washbowl

To the right of the door in the West Cloister can be seen a ledge; this was the monks' washing place or *lavatorium*. On this would have stood a trough, probably of lead, where the monks washed their hands before the meal and again afterwards. They ate with their hands, since forks were unknown until the later fourteenth century. Again, we can see how the roof supports of the later ceiling interrupt the earlier work.

Stone carving by the door of a man playing the bagpipes, perhaps a reminder to the monks of the everyday bustle that lay outside.

The round-headed door from the Cloister which leads to the steps into Abbey Square was the only access the monks had to the outside world. To the left of the door can be seen a man playing a drum, while on the other side is a man playing the bagpipes. The splendid door to the Refectory is a fine example of the Romanesque style and dates from about 1160; in the ceiling above the door is a boss showing the arms of Cardinal Wolsey, while to the right of the door is displayed the coat of arms of Henry VIII.

At the end of the East Cloister, leading to a staircase, is an unusually-shaped archway, which is neither round-headed nor as acutely pointed as later arches, and marks a transitional stage in the shift from Romanesque to Gothic in the late twelfth century. The stairs led up to the dormitory at first-floor level and are called the 'Day Stairs', since they would have been used for the first service of the day, 'Prime', which took place at sunrise. A new Song School, providing practice rooms for the choirs, office space, and music and robe storage, has recently been built on the site of the dormitory.

A passage called the 'Slype' (a variant of 'slip', in the sense of a covered narrow passageway) runs from east to west under the Song School. This formed the lay entrance to the monastery and, since visitors were met here, speech was allowed in this area. These passages are sometimes called 'parlours' from the French *parler*, to talk; in some monasteries, the prior even set up his office in this area.

A visitor to the monastery would then enter the Vestibule, beyond which lies the Chapter House. The Vestibule has a relatively low ceiling, supported by columns which run up into the ceiling without capitals (a band of decoration around the top of a column), giving a very graceful appearance and the impression of a much higher room.

The Chapter House, dating from the 1260s, is a magnificent example of Early English Gothic architecture, with particularly fine stone vaulting. Here the monks met daily to discuss the business affairs of the monastery, which owned estates all over the country. Before they began work the monks listened to a chapter from the Rule of St Benedict, hence the name Chapter House and, today, the 'Dean and Chapter'. It was the completion of the Chapter House in the Gothic style that prompted the monks to start rebuilding their Romanesque church in the new style.

The colourful East Window, installed in 1872, shows the history of the building as Anglo–Saxon minster, Benedictine monastery and cathedral. It is a superb example of Victorian stained glass craftsmanship, by Heaton, Butler & Bayne.

The beautifully proportioned Vestibule, with its elegant early Gothic columns.

The Chapter House window, installed in 1872 and restored in 2008.

The monastic Refectory, still in use today as the Cathedral's restaurant, for meetings, receptions and dinners.

Refectory

The present Refectory, or dining hall, still serves its original purpose. It dates from the mid thirteenth century but there must have been an earlier hall, for its Romanesque door still forms the main entrance from the Cloisters today. Extra windows were added in the fifteenth century and these can be recognised by their flatter 'Tudor' arches.

The monks took all their meals here, at tables raised on low platforms to recall the Last Supper. Conversation was forbidden; instead one of the monks read out suitable portions of the lives of the saints or other homilies from the magnificent wall-pulpit, a truly remarkable survival. The abbot sat on the raised dais at the far end of the room, with his important guests on either side of him — and they could be very important indeed. Several kings of England have eaten here, notably Edward I and Richard II, who loved the city so much that he styled himself 'Prince of Chester'.

Schoolboy graffiti

To the left of the East Window can be seen a name, Joseph Saunders, and the date 1689 carved in the wall. After the monastery was dissolved, the Refectory became the King's School – still in existence today; this is an early example of schoolboy graffiti!

Left: The Day Stairs, which originally led up to the dormitory; today they give access to the modern Song School.

The early twentieth-century East Window portrays the Saxon monarchs and saints who influenced the early history of the monastery, with St Werburgh in the centre, holding the Cathedral in her hand. The background of the window is formed by a tree, a symbol of the royal and saintly family. At the bottom of the window, on the left, is shown the great feast given when St Werburgh entered the abbey of Ely and the fair which used to be held in Chester on her feast day. Higher up on the right, the saint hangs her veil on a sunbeam. On either side are scenes from the history of her shrine.

The tapestry over the servery was woven at the Mortlake tapestry works in the early seventeenth century, one of a set designed by Raphael in 1515 for the Sistine Chapel. Until 1843 it hung at the east end of the Quire as the reredos to the High Altar. It shows St Paul in a celebrated scene with the sorcerer Elymas in Cyprus on his first missionary journey, when he strikes Elymas with temporary blindness for trying to prevent the proconsul Sergius Paulus from accepting the Christian faith.

The Refectory pulpit, one of the finest examples in the country; from it lessons were read while the monks ate in silence.

The roof dates from as recently as 1939, when it was decided to recreate the high-pitched roof of a medieval hall such as the great roof of Westminster Hall, but using modern building technology to speed the process, which took just six months. The roof is made of steel, with an oak ceiling beneath, and boards and slates above. The gables at each end of the room had to be raised to accommodate the increased pitch, and the fourteenth-century corbels, including two that were found elsewhere, were reused and some new ones carved to replace those lost. The richly decorated ceiling, both carved and painted, includes the coats of arms of people and places associated with the Cathedral, the monograms of residential and Minor Canons and the initials of individual craftsmen and firms involved in the construction. The iconography forms a short-hand history of the development of the building from early times.

The West or 'Creation' Window was installed in 2001 to commemorate the millennium. Designed and made by Rosalind Grimshaw, it is truly one of the treasures of Chester Cathedral. Each of the upper lights represents one of the six days of creation, while the lower panels have a mostly scientific connection and give a modern take on the subjects and images in the upper lights. Above the four central lights is the dove, representing the Holy Spirit, and reaching over the whole window is the Hand of God, creating and blessing. These images are made of prismatic glass, to refract and reflect light into the Refectory beneath.

Chester Cathedral
Looking Forward

The Cathedral continues to play a key role for the Christian community in the city of Chester, the county of Cheshire, and the diocese of Chester, which includes Wirral, Stockport, and parts of Warrington, Tameside and Trafford. It is a place of gathering, enabling large groups to celebrate, to commemorate and to worship together lying at the heart of the ancient city, it is also a focus for charitable causes; an education centre for young visitors; a centre of musical excellence; and a site of extraordinary historical significance which draws visitors from all over the world.

Requiring £1,000,000 a year to maintain, heat and light, the Cathedral is funded entirely independently, through the activities and endeavours of the cathedral community. It serves as a unique venue for large-scale functions and hospitality, while the Refectory offers the visitor the opportunity to eat a meal in exactly the same spot as that used by the 13th-century monks.

A special concert for schools in the Cathedral.

Learning in Chester Cathedral

Education is an important part of the Cathedral's mission; the Education Department welcomes over 7000 children and young people a year for interactive tours and educational activities. These are mainly school groups but they also include youth clubs and uniformed organisations. The Education Department also arranges visits for foreign-language students. Educational events include the annual Pilgrim Days (when 800–900 children come into the Cathedral over a period of a week) and an annual sixth form conference. There is also a thriving and growing Sunday school, which meets in term-time during the Sunday morning Eucharist.

Adult education is another important facet of the Cathedral's life, and includes bible talks, Lent and Advent groups and occasional lectures. A variety of guided tours are also available to adult visitors, including the opportunity to visit the Cathedral Library and discover some of its treasures.

A Living Musical Heritage

The English choral tradition is the lifeblood that turns our Cathedrals from silent spaces into resounding places of glory. Singing eight choral services each week, shared between the boy and girl choristers and the lay clerks, Chester Cathedral Choir sings some of the greatest music from the fourteenth century to the present day. The Cathedral Choir and the Nave Choir (the longest serving Cathedral voluntary choir in the country) rehearse weekly in the purpose-built Song School, which stands on the site of the monks' dormitory. In addition to the daily worship of the Cathedral, the Choir perform at least three concerts a year, record CDs and regularly appear on radio and television and, when time permits, undertake tours to other countries.

There is no choir school at Chester and the choristers are recruited from schools all over the city and surrounding area. The Cathedral itself provides bursaries for the choristers and this level of support, together with the commitment of the choir members, is absolutely vital to ensure consistently high musical standards.

Chester Cathedral plays proud host to the most extensive series of organ recitals in the country, with a weekly Thursday recital throughout the year. Recitalists from all over the world come here to perform, along with the Cathedral's own organists. Originally built by the Chester firm of Charles Whiteley in 1876, the organ enjoys a worldwide reputation as one of the finest in the country.

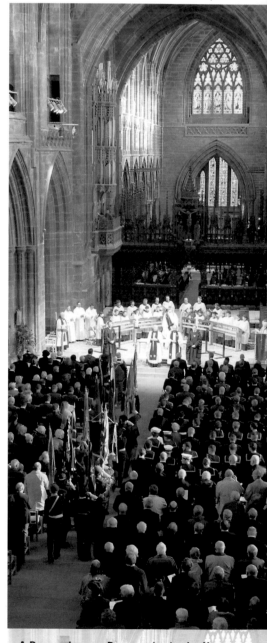

A Remembrance Day service in the Nave.